D1275626

SPIDERS

TARANTULA SPIDERS

James E. Gerholdt
ABDO & Daughters

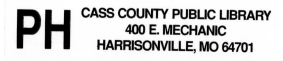

Published by Abdo & Daughters, 4940 Viking Drive, Suite 622, Edina, Minnesota 55435.

Library bound edition distributed by Rockbottom Books, Pentagon Tower, P.O. Box 36036, Minneapolis, Minnesota 55435.

Printed in the United States.

Cover Photo credit: Peter Arnold, Inc.
Interior Photo credits: Peter Arnold, Inc. pages 13, 15, 17, 19
James Gerholdt pages 5, 7, 9, 11, 21
Pages 7 & 11 courtesy of Black Hills Reptile Gardens.
Pages 7, 11, 21 courtesy of Spineless Wonders.

Edited by Julie Berg

Library of Congress Cataloging-in-Publication Data

Gerholdt, James E., 1943
     Tarantula / James E. Gerholdt.
       p. cm. — (Spiders)
Includes bibliographical references (p.23) and Index.
  ISBN 1-56239-506-8
1. Tarantulas—Juvenile literature. [1. Tarantulas. 2. Spiders.] I. Title. II. Series:
Gerholdt, James E., 1943 Spiders.
QL458.42.T5G47 1995
595.4'4—dc20
                                     95-13010
                                     CIP
                                     AC

About the Author

Jim Gerholdt has been studying reptiles and amphibians for more than 40 years. He has presented lectures and displays throughout the state of Minnesota for 9 years. He is a founding member of the Minnesota Herpetological Society and is active in conservation issues involving reptiles and amphibians in India and Aruba, as well as Minnesota.

Contents

TARANTULAS

Tarantulas belong to one of the 84 spider **families**. A spider is an **arachnid**. It has two body parts and eight legs. All arachnids are **arthropods**. Their skeletons are on the outside of their bodies. Tarantulas are also **ectothermic**. They get their body temperature from the **environment**.

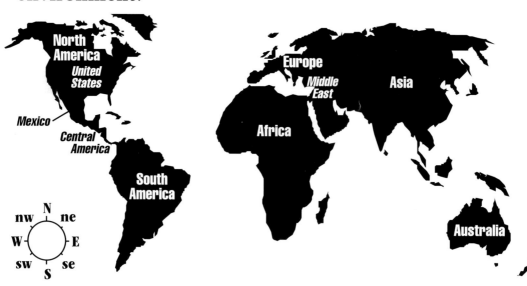

Tarantulas are found in Africa, Europe, the Middle East, Asia, South and Central America, Mexico and the southwestern United States.

The Chilean flame tarantula is large and hairy.

There are about 37,000 **species** of spiders in the world. About 800 of these are tarantulas and bird-eaters. The name *tarantula* comes from Taranto, a seaport in southern Italy, where the spider is commonly found. They are large, hairy spiders with fangs that strike down.

SIZES

Tarantulas are large spiders. The king baboon spider from Africa can be over three inches (8 cm) long with legs measuring almost 10 inches (26 cm) across. The colorful Mexican orange-knee tarantula can have a **legspan** of over five inches (13 cm).

While not as large, many other tarantulas have a body length of three inches (8 cm) and a legspan of five inches (13 cm). Small **species**, like some of the pink-toed tarantulas, may have a body length of less than $1^1/_2$ inches (4 cm).

The king baboon spider from Africa is one of the largest spiders in the world.

SHAPES

Tarantulas are very heavy-bodied. They are also very hairy! They have two body parts that are almost round in shape. The head and **thorax** make up the **cephalothorax**. The rear body part is called the **abdomen**. It contains the **spinnerets** which make the spider's silk.

Eight legs are attached to the front of the body, along with the **pedipalps**, which look like two short legs.

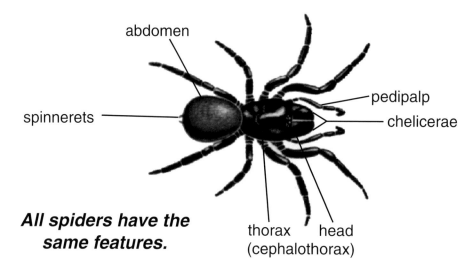

All spiders have the same features.

The pedipalps can be seen on this tarantula from South America.

Spiders use these to grab their **prey**. Between the **pedipalps** are the **chelicerae**, to which the fangs are attached.

COLORS

Tarantulas come in many different colors. Most, like the Chilean common tarantula, are completely brown. Other **species**, like the Mexican orange-knee tarantula, are black or dark brown, with orange on the legs and the **cephalothorax**.

The tiger rump tarantula from Costa Rica is black with a reddish cephalothorax and stripes on the **abdomen**. The Asian species, like the ornamental **rainforest** tarantula, are patterned.

The Mexican orange-knee tarantula is one of the most colorful of all the tarantulas.

WHERE THEY LIVE

Tarantulas are found in many different kinds of **habitats**. Some **species**, like the Mexican blond tarantula, live in dry, desert **scrubland**. They are found in Mexico, Arizona, and Texas. Other species, such as the East African horned baboon, live in the East African **rainforests**. Many of the Central and South American species also like habitats where the **humidity** is high.

Some species live in **burrows** which may be lined with silk from the **spinnerets**. Others live in trees, where they make a silken tube in which to hide. Species that live under tree bark may line their hideaway with silk. Others will make a silken spot on which to lay.

This tarantula is crawling out of its burrow. It lives in the tropical forest of Costa Rica.

SENSES

Tarantulas have the same five senses as humans. Like most spiders, they have eight eyes. But the eyesight of a tarantula is not very sharp. Most **species** are active at night, so their eyes are used to detect light levels.

The hairs on the tarantula's legs and **pedipalps** are sensitive to **vibrations**. They help the spider feel its way along its path.

Spiders also smell and taste the world around them. Tarantulas can taste with their mouth, and with the ends of the pedipalps and legs.

This is the head of a tarantula. Although they have eight eyes, their eyesight is not very sharp.

DEFENSE

Many tarantulas use **camouflage** to defend themselves against enemies. Even some of the bright colored **species** are difficult to see in their **habitats**.

If the camouflage doesn't work, the tarantula may rear back and frighten away the **predator**. Tarantulas also will bite! While the bite isn't usually dangerous to humans, it can be painful.

Tarantulas can defend themselves by shedding their hairs. The hairs are very irritating to the skin of a human or a predator. They are also a major problem for the predator if the hairs get into the eyes.

Tarantulas bite enemies with their fangs. Although the bite can be fatal to their prey, it is usually not dangerous to humans.

FOOD

A hungry tarantula is a fearsome creature. It is an active hunter and will eat any animal it can overpower. Its **prey** may be insects, other spiders, frogs, lizards, snakes, and birds.

The tarantula grabs prey with its **pedipalps**. It bites the prey and holds on until the poison from the fangs kills the victim. Then the tarantula sucks out all the fluids. All that is left of the prey is a shapeless mass!

This tarantula from Brazil is climbing a branch in search of food.

BABIES

All tarantulas hatch from eggs that have been laid by the female. They are laid in an egg case that she builds and guards. The baby spiders hatch in two weeks to three months. Without the proper heat and **humidity**, the eggs will not hatch.

After the eggs hatch, the baby spiders often stay near the female. But soon they go their own way.

As they grow, the spiders shed their skins. This is called **moulting**. The shed skin looks much like the spider from which it came. It is often hard to tell which is the spider and which is the skin!

A baby Mexican orange-knee tarantula.

GLOSSARY

Abdomen (AB-do-men) - The rear body part of an arachnid.

Arachnid (uh-RACK-nid) - An arthropod with two body parts and eight legs.

Arthropod (ARTH-row-pod) - An animal with its skeleton on the outside of its body.

Burrow - A hole in the ground dug by an animal; also, to dig a burrow.

Camouflage (CAM-a-flaj) - The ability to blend in with the surroundings.

Cephalothorax (seff-uh-luh-THOR-ax) - The front body part of an arachnid.

Chelicerae (kel-ISS-err-eye) - The leg-like organs of a spider that have fangs attached to them.

Ectothermic (ek-toe-THERM-ik) - Regulating body temperature from an outside source.

Environment (en-VI-ron-ment) - Surroundings in which an animal lives.

Family (FAM-i-lee) - A grouping of animals.

Habitat (HAB-uh-tat) - An area in which an animal lives.

Humidity - The amount of water in the air.

Legspan - The distance between the tips of opposite leg pairs on a spider.

Moulting (MOLE-ting) - The act of shedding old skin.

Pedipalps (PED-uh-palps) - The two, long sense organs on the head of an arachnid.

Predator (PRED-uh-tore) - An animal that eats other animals.

Prey - Animals that are eaten by other animals.
Rainforest - A dense, tropical forest that gets lots of rain.
Scrubland - An area with low, stunted trees or shrubs.
Species (SPEE-seas) - A kind or type.
Spinnerets (spin-er-ETS) - The two body parts attached to the abdomen of a spider where the silk is made.
Thorax (THORE-axe) - Part of the front body of an arachnid.
Vibration (vie-BRAY-shun) - Rapid movement up and down or back and forth.

BIBLIOGRAPHY

de Vosjoli, Philippe. *Arachnomania - The General Care and Maintenance of Tarantulas and Scorpions.* Advanced Vivarium Systems, 1991.

Levi, Herbert W. and Lorna R. *Spiders and Their Kin.* Golden Press, 1990.

O'Toole, Christopher (editor). *The Encyclopedia of Insects.* Facts on File, Inc., 1986.

Preston-Mafham, Rod and Ken. *Spiders of the World.* Facts on File, Inc., 1984.

Webb, Ann. *The Proper Care of Tarantulas.* T.F.H. Publications, Inc., 1992.

Index